D1406564

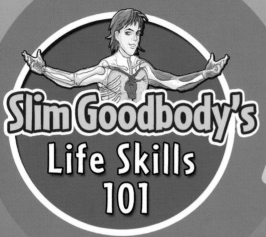

Slim Goodbody's Life Skills 101

MANNERS, PLEASE!

Why It Pays to Be Polite

CRABTREE
Publishing Company
www.crabtreebooks.com

Crabtree Publishing Company
www.crabtreebooks.com

Series Development, Writing, and Packaging:
John Burstein, Slim Goodbody Corp.

Editors:
Lynn Peppas
Valerie Weber, Wordsmith Ink.

Editorial director:
Kathy Middleton

Production coordinator:
Ken Wright

Prepress technician:
Ken Wright

Designer:
Tammy West, Westgraphix LLC.

Photos:
Chris Pinchback, Pinchback Photography

Photo credits:
© Creative Commons: page 7 (top)
© iStock Photos: pages 2, 6, 7 (bottom), 12, 27, 28, 29 (top)
© Slim Goodbody: pages 1, 4, 5, 8, 9, 10, 11, 13, 14, 15, 16, 17, 18, 19, 20, 21, 22, 23, 24, 25, 26, 29 (except top)

Acknowledgements:
The author would like to thank the following people for their help in this project:
Christine Burstein, Lucas Burstein, Tristan Fong, Jessie Goodale, Adriana Goodale, Colby Hill, Ginny Laurita, Louis Laurita, Renaissance Lyman, Jack Henry Grannis-Phoenix, Ariel Power, Joah Welt

"Slim Goodbody" and Pinchback photos, copyright, © Slim Goodbody

"Slim Goodbody" and "Slim Goodbody's Life Skills 101" are registered trademarks of the Slim Goodbody Corp.

Library and Archives Canada Cataloguing in Publication

Burstein, John
  Manners, please! : why it pays to be polite / John Burstein.

(Slim Goodbody's life skills 101)
Includes index.
Issued also in an electronic format.
ISBN 978-0-7787-4795-6 (bound).--ISBN 978-0-7787-4811-3 (pbk.)

  1. Etiquette--Juvenile literature. I. Title. II. Title: Why it pays to be polite. III. Series: Burstein, John. Slim Goodbody's life skills 101.

BJ1857.C5B87 2010   j395.1'22   C2010-902761-2

Library of Congress Cataloging-in-Publication Data

Burstein, John.
  Manners, please! why it pays to be polite / [John Burstein].
    p. cm. -- (Slim Goodbody's life skills 101)
  Includes index.
  ISBN 978-0-7787-4811-3 (pbk. : alk. paper) -- ISBN 978-0-7787-4795-6
(reinforced library binding : alk. paper) -- ISBN 978-1-4271-9533-3
(electronic (pdf))
  1. Etiquette for children and teenagers. I. Title. II. Series.

BJ1857.C5B87 2011
395.1'22--dc22
                                2010016403

Crabtree Publishing Company
www.crabtreebooks.com   1-800-387-7650

Printed in China/082010/AP20100512

Published in Canada
Crabtree Publishing
616 Welland Ave.
St. Catharines, Ontario
L2M 5V6

Published in the United States
Crabtree Publishing
PMB 59051
350 Fifth Avenue, 59th Floor
New York, New York 10118

Published in the United Kingdom
Crabtree Publishing
Maritime House
Basin Road North, Hove
BN41 1WR

Published in Australia
Crabtree Publishing
386 Mt. Alexander Rd.
Ascot Vale (Melbourne)
VIC 3032

CONTENTS

Words in **bold** are defined in the glossary on page 30.

DO MANNERS MATTER?

Tammy and Corinne were excited about the class trip to the museum.

"I can't wait to see the Tyrannosaurus Rex," said Tammy.

"I wish we could ride it," laughed Corinne.

When the bus arrived at the museum, Corrine started pushing past the other kids. "Let's get in first," she said.

"I'll wait my turn," said Tammy as she watched Corrine charge ahead.

Outside, her teacher took Corrine aside. "Corrine, we don't push others in the class," Mr. Carver said. "It's rude, and it isn't safe." When Corrine didn't reply, he added, "I've spoken to you about your behavior before. Please go to the end of the line."

Corrine stomped off to the back of the line. As she passed her classmates, she noticed that some seemed happy about her punishment. She felt even more upset.

Tammy felt sorry for Corinne. She asked her teacher, "May I please go to the back of the line, too?" Mr. Carver replied, "Since you've asked so politely, go right ahead."

Corinne whispered to Tammy, "Why is Mr. Carver always so nice to you but not to me? And some of the kids in the class aren't nice to me either."

"Maybe it's your manners," Tammy replied.

Corrine glared at her and snapped, "Manners don't matter. There's nothing wrong with trying to get ahead of the crowd. That's the way to become a leader."

Tammy didn't know what to say.

Hi. My name is Slim Goodbody.

When you treat other people with respect and **consideration**, you're practicing good manners. Your manners say a lot about the kind of person you are. They show whether you care about other people's feelings or not. They show if you are a generous person or a selfish one.

People with good manners tend to be successful in life because they get along better with others. People with good manners treat others with respect. In return, others treat them with respect.

A LITTLE HISTORY

People have been concerned with good manners throughout history. For example:

- *The Instructions of Ptahhote* is a 4,000-year-old list of manners. Scientists believe Ptahhote served an Egyptian **pharaoh** and wrote these instructions for the pharaoh's son.

- Over 2,000 years ago, the ancient Greeks and Romans wrote books about manners.

- In 1746 when George Washington was fourteen, he copied out a list of manners from a book. He called his list "*Rules of **Civility**.*"

Times Change

Good manners never go out of style, but they do change over time. For example, no one follows this bit of advice from a book on manners written by Daniel of Beccles in the 1200s: "Don't mount your horse in the hall." Many other manners have changed as well. For example, during the 1600s, children were supposed to

- stand when adults entered the room and offer their seats;
- bow or **curtsy** when they met adults;
- keep quiet in front of adults unless spoken to.

Manners Change from Place to Place

People who live in different countries do not have the same manners. In some countries, it is **impolite** to wave hello with your palm facing out. In some countries, it is perfectly polite to eat meals on the floor and use your fingers to eat.

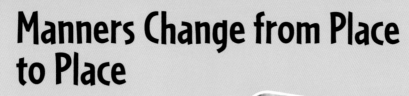

Puzzled?

You may be thinking that manners can be pretty confusing. Luckily, a general rule holds true in almost all **situations**. If you understand how this rule works, you can develop excellent manners.

The most helpful guide for manners is called the Golden Rule. It has been around for hundreds of years and has been said in many ways. One way is,"Treat others as you want others to treat you." Another is, "Love your neighbor as yourself."

All of us want to be treated with respect and consideration. If you show consideration for others, they are more likely to show consideration for you. If you respect others, you lead them to act in the same way toward you.

A User-friendly Rule

The Golden Rule is a very practical and **user-friendly** guide. You can use it in all kinds of situations to help you behave well. If you're not sure what to do, ask yourself, "How would I want others to treat me if I were in their place?" Here are some examples:

- Would I want to be left out of a game?
- Would I be happy if someone cut ahead of me in a line?
- Would I be upset if someone took something of mine without asking?
- What if someone borrowed something from me and didn't say "Thank you"?

If you would feel unhappy to be treated in certain ways by others, then don't treat *them* that way.

Turn It Around

The Golden Rule is especially important when someone treats you unkindly. For example, suppose someone calls you a bad name. If you respond by calling him or her a bad name, it can lead to a fight. But remember the Golden Rule and think about how you would like to be treated. Then you might respond by saying, "No one likes being called names. Please cut it out." If you walk away afterward, you've made your point and stopped the name-calling.

TRY EMPATHY

To apply the Golden Rule, it helps to have **empathy** for other people. Empathy is trying to understand or imagine another person's feelings.

  Suppose a friend of yours is angry. You would be showing empathy if you could honestly say something like, "I understand how you feel right now. You are so frustrated and angry. I would be too, if I were in your situation." Empathy means *feeling with* a person, instead of *feeling sorry for* a person.

An Important Goal

If you can empathize with how others feel, you are less likely to do something to hurt their feelings. For example, imagine that you and a friend are on the same soccer team. In the last moments of a big game, your friend misses a goal that would have won the game.

If you want to show empathy, start by thinking how you would feel if you had missed the shot. Then you'll have a much better idea of how your friend might be feeling.

Next consider which of the following two statements you would rather hear from your friend. Think about why you would want one statement over another:

- "Sorry you missed the goal. We could have won."

- "I know how you must feel. I've missed some important goals, too. I had to remind myself that I tried my best. You did too."

I think you'll agree that the second statement expresses empathy. Your friend will feel you truly understand what he or she is feeling.

MAGIC WORDS

When you were younger, your parents may have taught you some "magic words," such as:

- **Please**
- **Thank you**
- **You're welcome**
- **Excuse me**
- **I'm sorry**

Do you think these words are really magical? Of course they aren't. But these magic words can cast a powerful spell. They can instantly change the way someone thinks of you or what you are doing. For example:

- "Please" can magically turn a demand into a request.
- "Thank you" is a charm that changes sour feelings to sweet ones.
- "I'm sorry" can heal hurt feelings.

Politeness Pays

When you are polite to others, you show that you appreciate what they do for you. When people feel appreciated, they are more likely to come to your aid the next time you need help.

Sign Language

Here is how those magic words are expressed in sign language:

• **Please:** With your right hand flat and facing your chest, make a circle to the left over the center of your chest.

• **Thank you:** Touch your chin or lips with the fingertips of one flat hand, then move your hand forward until your palm is facing up. The hand moves out and down.

• **You're welcome:** The sign is done by holding the flat hand palm up out away from your body (off to the right a bit) and then bringing the hand in toward your body. You can nod your head a bit and smile.

• **Excuse me:** Hold your left hand palm up. Holding all right fingertips together, move fingers of your right hand from the heel to the tip of the left hand. The movement looks like you're wiping away a mistake.

• **I'm sorry:** The hand shape for the letter A circles the center of your chest to show that you're feeling sad. Your closed hand faces your body.

A COUPLE OF CHARACTERS

I want you to meet two **imaginary** characters. I call them Rufus and Myrtle. They'll show us how manners, or the lack of manners, matter in different situations.

Rufus: Bathroom Hog

Rufus wakes up and goes into the bathroom to wash his face and brush his teeth. He's a little tired and moves very slowly. Outside the door, his sister Carla calls, "Please hurry up. I don't want to be late for school." Rufus answers, "Get lost, Carla. You'll just have to wait till I'm done." Rufus moves extra slowly to keep his sister waiting.

Off to School

After breakfast, Rufus yells, "I'm leaving!" and slams the door shut. Outside, he sees a man walking a dog. "Cool dog," Rufus thinks. He reaches down to pat the pooch, but the dog growls. Rufus snatches his hand away. Giving the man an angry look, he says, "Stupid dog," and hurries away.

As he rounds the corner, Rufus sees the school bus about to leave. "Wait for me," he yells and begins to run. Luckily, the bus driver sees him and waits. Rufus slows down and walks the rest of the way to the bus. He gets on, walks past the driver, and sits down.

Figure It Out

In this story, there are eight times Rufus could have used good manners but didn't. Can you figure out what those times were? Consider the Golden Rule. Ask yourself if Rufus showed respect and consideration for others. Did Rufus treat his sister or the bus driver as he would like to be treated? The answers are printed upside down on the bottom of the page.

MYRTLE ON THE BUS

Myrtle hates to be late. She always wants to be first into school. So when her bus arrives, she cuts in front of everyone in line. When the bus arrives at school, Myrtle rushes to get off in front of everyone.

And in School

Myrtle sees her classmate Mara going through the door into school. "I can't let her beat me," Myrtle thinks. Speeding toward the door, she notices someone carrying a science project. "Get out of my way," Myrtle says.

Running down the hall, Myrtle passes the hall **monitor**. "Please, slow down!" calls the monitor. But Myrtle ignores her. When she reaches her classroom, Mara is just ahead of her. Myrtle speeds past her teacher who is standing at the door.

"Slow down, Myrtle," her teacher says. Myrtle pays no attention to her teacher. But it's too late. Mara sits down. As Myrtle heads for her seat, she picks up a pretty pencil from someone's desk. "I'll borrow this and give it back later," she tells herself.

Myrtle sits down and checks to be sure her teacher isn't watching. Then she sticks her tongue out at Mara.

Myrtle is furious. Every time Mara raises her hand to answer a question, Myrtle yells out an answer. "I'll show her!" Myrtle thinks.

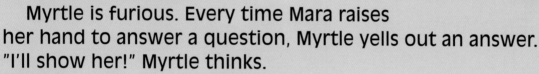

Figure It Out

In this story, Myrtle showed poor manners seven times. Before you read the answers below, try to come up with them yourself. Suppose you were Myrtle's friend. How would you help her see the value of the Golden Rule?

ANSWERS

1. Myrtle cut in line at the bus stop. 2. Myrtle didn't hold the door for the person holding the science project. 3. Myrtle didn't listen to the hall monitor. 4. Myrtle ignored her teacher. 5. Myrtle borrowed the pencil without asking the owner. 6. Myrtle stuck her tongue out at Mara. 7. Myrtle **interrupted** the class.

RETURN TO RUFUS: IN THE LUNCHROOM

Rufus is starving. They are serving spaghetti, one of Rufus's favorites. In the lunch line, people seem to be moving in slow motion! He pushes his tray against the kid in front of him, trying to speed things along. Finally he gets his lunch and goes to sit down with his friends.

The seat next to Rufus is empty. But when Sam, the new kid, tries to sit down, Rufus says, "Seat taken!" Another boy at the table says, "Hi Sam, it's OK. You can join us." Sam sits down.

Rufus, takes a huge bite of spaghetti. Some strands hang down across his chin, so he sucks them in loudly. With sauce smeared on his chin, Rufus looks over at Sam. "Boy, you have some funny-looking food," laughs Rufus, as he chews with his mouth open. "It looks like mush."

Rufus then burps loudly and laughs. When the meal is over, Sam carries his leftovers to the garbage can. As Sam walks away, Rufus looks at his friends. He whispers loudly, "Don't let him eat with us again."

When the bell rings, Rufus gets up. "No time to clean up now," he tells himself as he leaves the lunchroom.

Figure It Out

There are nine examples of poor manners in this story. Which of these manners goes against the Golden Rule? How so? Does Rufus show empathy toward others?

ANSWERS

1. Rufus pushed the tray into the person ahead of him. 2. Rufus didn't offer Sam a seat even though there was room at the table. 3. Rufus stuffed his mouth full. 4. Rufus slurped his food. 5. Rufus talked with his mouth full. 6. Rufus made fun of Sam's food. 7. Rufus burped at the table. 8. Rufus talked about Sam behind his back. 9. Rufus didn't take responsibility for keeping the lunchroom clean.

MYRTLE ON THE COURT

Myrtle's basketball team is playing a big game against another school. As always, Myrtle wants to come in first. She just can't stand to lose.

When Myrtle gets the ball, she races down the court. One of her teammates waves and yells, "I'm free." But Myrtle won't pass. She wants to score the basket herself. Myrtle doesn't think anyone else on the team is as good as she is. She shoots and scores. She yells at the other team, "Losers!"

The next time that Myrtle gets the ball, it's stolen away. Myrtle races after the girl who stole the ball and shoves her.

The **referee** calls a **penalty**. Myrtle yells at the referee, "I didn't do anything. You're not fair!" Her coach says, "Myrtle, please calm down."

Later one of Myrtle's teammates misses a shot. Myrtle yells, "You can't shoot. You should have passed it to me!" The next time that same teammate shoots, she scores. Myrtle doesn't say a word.

A Poor Sport

Myrtle's team plays hard, but the other team begins to rack up points. Myrtle becomes **discouraged**. "We'll never win, so why bother?" she tells herself and stops running hard.

The game is over, and the two teams line up to shake hands. Myrtle shakes hands but glares angrily at everyone. She refuses to say, "Good game."

Figure It Out

Can you figure out nine examples of poor manners?

BACK TO RUFUS: PHONE MANNERS

Rufus arrives home just in time to hear the phone ringing. He answers it, saying, "Yeah?" The person on the phone asks, "Hello, is this Rufus?" "Duh! Who do think it is?" replies Rufus. "This is Shawna. May I speak to Carla please?" "Hold on a second," Rufus says. He yells to his sister at the top of his lungs, "CARLA!" When no one answers, Rufus says, "She's not here. Call back later." Then Rufus hangs up.

Rufus decides to call his friend Larry to invite him over. When Larry answers the phone, Rufus sneezes. Wiping his nose on the back of his hand, Rufus asks Larry, "Want to come to my house tomorrow? We can play some video games." Larry says that he'll ask his mom.

Rufus says, "OK. Hey, let me tell you about this video game we'll play!"

While Rufus is talking, Carla comes home. She says hello, but Rufus doesn't notice. "Please let me know when you're off the phone," says Carla. "I have to make an important call." Rufus nods his head yes. Fifteen minutes later, Rufus hangs up and goes to his room to play his new video game.

Figure It Out

There are eight examples of bad manners in this story. Can you figure them out?

ANSWERS

1. Rufus didn't say "Hello" when he answered the phone. 2. Rufus didn't cover the phone before yelling for someone to come and get it. 3. Rufus didn't take a message and write it down. 4. Rufus hung up without saying "Good-bye." 5. Rufus sneezed on the receiver. 6. Rufus didn't ask his friend what he wanted to do. 7. Rufus hogged the phone. 8. Rufus didn't tell his sister that he was finished with the phone or give her a message.

MYRTLE AT DINNER

Myrtle comes home from the basketball game just as dinner is about to be served. She races to the table and sits down. Her brother is just about to pick up a burrito. "Yum," says Myrtle and reaches across to grab one first. She is chewing away just as the rest of the family is sitting down.

The burrito drips a bit and gets Myrtle's hands a little greasy. "My basketball uniform is already dirty," she thinks to herself. So she wipes her hands on her shorts.

There is a bowl of rice on the table. The rice looks so good that Myrtle has to have some right away. She jabs her spoon into the bowl and fills it full. Then she eats the rice off her spoon and jabs it

right back into the rice for another mouthful. She shovels the rice in at lightning speed. She pays no attention to what anyone is saying.

When Myrtle finally looks up, she notices the burritos are almost gone! She grabs the last one and wolfs it down. When Myrtle is finally full, she gets up and leaves the table.

Figure It Out

Can you identify the ten examples of bad manners in this story?

1. Myrtle didn't wash her hands before coming to the table. 2. Myrtle didn't wait for everyone to sit down before eating. 3. Myrtle didn't say "Thank you" for the food. 4. Myrtle didn't use a napkin to clean her hands. 5. Myrtle didn't ask for food to be passed. 6. Myrtle fed herself right from the bowl of rice instead of putting the rice on her plate. 7. Myrtle ignored everyone at the table. 8. Myrtle grabbed the last burrito without checking to be sure others had their share. 9. Myrtle didn't ask to be excused from the table. 10. Myrtle didn't ask if she could help clear the dishes.

RUFUS AND MYRTLE WITH FRIENDS

Rufus opens the door. "You're late!" he tells Larry. "I'm sorry, Rufus." Rufus shrugs, "I started without you. Now you have to wait until I finish."

Rufus takes almost thirty minutes before he turns to Larry and says, "OK, let's play." Larry says, "I'm a little thirsty." Rufus groans, "I'll get you something to drink later. Stop being such a dork."

When the game is over, Rufus tells Larry it's time for him to go. Larry calls his dad for a ride while Rufus goes back to playing his game. He says, "See you, Larry. You can find the door, can't you?"

Figure It Out

In this story, there are six examples of poor manners. Can you identify them?

ANSWERS

1. Rufus didn't make Larry feel welcome by saying "Hello." 2. Rufus kept Larry waiting while he played. 3. When Larry was thirsty, Rufus didn't get him something to drink. 4. Rufus called Larry a bad name. 5. Rufus rudely told Larry to go home. 6. Rufus didn't walk with Larry to the door.

26

At the Movies

While waiting for the movie to start, Myrtle tells her friend Madison about the basketball game. When the movie starts, Myrtle keeps right on talking until she finishes the story.

Then Myrtle tears open a big bag of chips. Each time she reaches in to grab a handful, the bag crinkles loudly. When she's done, she crunches up the bag and drops it on the floor.

Myrtle's cell phone rings, and she answers it, speaking loudly. As Myrtle watches the movie, she keeps commenting on it. Every few minutes, she says something like, "I bet I know what's going to happen."

Figure It Out

Can you identify the five examples of bad manners in this story?

NO ONE'S PERFECT

I'm sure you aren't as poorly behaved as Rufus and Myrtle. But I'll bet that there are some things that they do that you—or your friends—may do as well. For example:

- Do you ever make fun of people?

- Do you ever have friends over and make them do what you want?

No one has perfect manners. However, we can all improve if we try.

Imagine

You are old enough by now to understand that there is a lot of fighting in this world. Many people find it hard to get along with each other. This leads to terrible arguments, hatred, and even war.

Imagine how different our world would be if everyone lived by the Golden Rule. Suppose everyone treated each other as they wished to be treated. Would people continue to hurt each other?

You may think changing the world is way too big a job for you to do. You are right and wrong. You certainly can't do it alone, but you can set a good example for others. If they follow your example, you can make your school or community more friendly and peaceful. If your school or community sets an example, other schools and communities will follow.

Imagine a stone dropped in a still pond. That one action creates ripples that keep spreading out. In this same way the Golden Rule's message of respect and consideration can spread until the whole world becomes a more peaceful place to live.

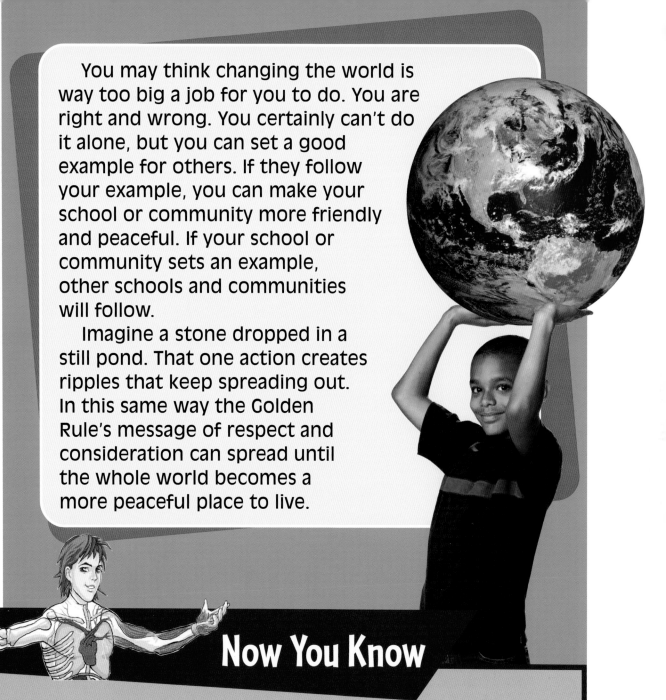

Now You Know

No one has perfect manners. However, we can all improve if we try. Practicing good manners is not about memorizing and obeying a lot of rules. It's trying to understand the goal behind the rules, so you can always act with respect for yourself and others.

Respectful attitudes, words, and actions will help you throughout your life. People will enjoy spending time with you. And they'll be much more likely to treat you well in return. Every day, you can make our world a little kinder and a little nicer place to live.

GLOSSARY

civility Courtesy, politeness, manners

consideration Careful thought for other people and their feelings

curtsy A short bow made by bending at the knee and lowering the body forward slightly to show respect; Girls curtsy and boys bow.

discouraged Having lost hope in something

empathy Understanding someone else's situation and feelings

imaginary Describing something that exists only in the mind

impolite Not polite, rude

interrupted Stopped a person from speaking or moving

monitor A person that warns or keeps watch. A hall monitor makes sure people move safely through a school.

penalty A punishment or disadvantage given to a player or team for breaking the rules in a sport

pharaoh A name given to kings in ancient Egypt

referee The person who makes sure a game is played fairly and enforces the rules

situations The way things are; conditions

user-friendly Easy to learn, understand, and use

BOOKS

Espeland, Pamela, and Elizabeth Verdick. *Dude, That's Rude!: (Get Some Manners)*. Free Spirit Publishing

Groves, Marsha. *Manners And Customs in the Middle Ages (Medieval World)* Crabtree Publishing Company

Leaf, Munro. *Manners Can Be Fun*. Universe

Senning, Cindy Post, and Peggy Post. *Emily Post's The Guide to Good Manners for Kids*. HarperCollins Children's Books

WEB SITES

Emily Post
*www.emilypost.com/kidsandparents/tip_cards/
    Table_Manners_web.pdf*
Click on this link to get a poster of the thirteen top table manners every kid should know.

KidsHealth
http://kidshealth.org/kid/feeling/emotion/good_sport.html
Explore this site to learn more about being a good sport, and find out how to spread the word to others.

Kids' Health
*www.cyh.com/HealthTopics/HealthTopicDetailsKids.aspx
    ?p=335&id=2526&np=287*
This Web site has a lot of information as well as kids' pictures and poems. Be sure to scroll to the bottom to find a link to download a manners poster from 1898!

Slim Goodbody
www.slimgoodbody.com
Discover loads of fun and free downloads for kids, teachers, and parents.

INDEX

About the Author
John Burstein (also known as Slim Goodbody) has been entertaining and educating children for over thirty years. His programs have been broadcast on CBS, PBS, Nickelodeon, USA, and Discovery. He has won numerous awards including the Parent's Choice Award and the President's Council's Fitness Leader Award. Currently, Mr. Burstein tours the country with his multimedia live show "Bodyology." For more information, please visit **slimgoodbody.com**.